D1712856

Sir
Walter Raleigh

by Madeline Boskey

Harcourt

Orlando   Austin   Chicago   New York   Toronto   London   San Diego

Visit *The Learning Site!*
www.harcourtschool.com

Sir Walter Raleigh

On a brisk fall day in 1618, a small crowd gathered in a courtyard in London, England. They were there to witness the death of Sir Walter Raleigh, one of the most famous men of his time. Raleigh had been a brave soldier, a daring explorer, and a smart businessperson. He had written books and had been a friend of the poet Edmund Spenser. He had even been made a knight by England's Queen Elizabeth I. Here is the story of his rise and fall.

Raleigh was born in 1554 in Devonshire, a county in England. He was the youngest son of a farmer. Raleigh's ancestors had lived in Devonshire for hundreds of years. At one time the family had owned a lot of land. When Walter was growing up, the Raleighs lost much of their money. They had to move from a large home to a simple farmhouse within Devonshire.

Devonshire, where Walter Raleigh grew up, is known for its mild climate, sunny days, and Dartmoor ponies.

Devonshire borders the English Channel, the body of water that separates England from France. Raleigh's father owned several ships. As a boy, Raleigh spent a lot of time listening to sailors tell about their travels. Their stories made him long to sail to places where no European had ever been.

Raleigh dreamed of setting off for faraway lands. In 1569 at the age of 17, he went to France. France was in the midst of a civil war in which Protestants fought against Roman Catholics. Raleigh joined the Protestant army.

By the time he was 18, Raleigh was studying at Oxford University. There he studied the voyages of famous explorers. One explorer who fascinated him was Hernando Cortés (1485–1547), who had conquered the Aztec Empire of Mexico for Spain. Another was Francisco Pizarro (1475–1541), a Spanish explorer who had conquered Peru.

Raleigh left Oxford in 1575 to go to the city of London to study law. Later he quit his law studies to go into business with his brothers. Their plan was to sail to North America and set up an English colony. The attempt failed, and their ships sailed back to England.

In 1580 Raleigh used his military skills in Ireland. He went there with 100 soldiers to help his brothers stop a revolt against English rule.

TEK
DID YOU KNOW

Time to Wear Pants!
In Raleigh's time, boys wore skirts until they were four to seven years old. At that age, they were given their first pair of breeches, or knee-length pants. This was an important occasion. Families marked the event, called a *breeching*, with a party. After being "breeched," boys were considered ready for the world.

Oxford University, which Sir Walter Raleigh attended, is more than 800 years old.

By this time, Raleigh was 26 years old. Reports say he was six feet (almost 2 m) tall—a giant in the 1500s, when people tended to be short. He was handsome, confident, and funny. He was even able to laugh at himself. He once wrote a book in jail. In the book's opening pages, he thanked his jailers. If he had not been imprisoned, he said, he wouldn't have "had this leisure, to have made myself a fool in print."

Queen Elizabeth's 45-year reign (1558–1603) was an exciting time. It has been called England's Golden Age. It was a time when England grew strong in many areas. Trade with other nations increased, as did the nation's military might. The theater and other arts thrived. Writers such as William Shakespeare created masterpieces. It was a time that offered many opportunities for ambitious men like Walter Raleigh.

Queen Elizabeth often met with members of Parliament to discuss life in England and its many colonies.

COC

captured Spanish vessels. Much of the gold and silver the Spanish ships carried became his. By the late 1580s, Raleigh was one of the richest and most powerful men in England. He was also one of the most adventurous.

Sailors from Italy, Portugal, and Spain were the first Europeans to reach the Americas. During the reign of Queen Elizabeth, the English wanted to expand overseas. As the shipbuilding industry grew, long-distance voyages became safer. English explorers, such as Sir Francis Drake, Sir Humphrey Gilbert, and Sir Walter Raleigh, began to explore across the Atlantic Ocean.

Raleigh spent a lot of his own money trying to start an English colony in North America. Queen Elizabeth wouldn't let him sail there. She didn't want to risk losing her adviser, but she encouraged him to organize voyages.

In 1584 Queen Elizabeth gave Raleigh the lands he claimed in the name of England.

Some of the ships he sent landed in what is now the state of North Carolina. Others explored the coast all the way to Florida. Raleigh named the entire area Virginia in honor of the queen. From 1584 to 1602, Raleigh arranged or helped pay for at least seven voyages to the region. He was unable to form any long-lasting settlement there.

When John White returned to Roanoke he found the word *CROATOAN* carved into wood. To this day, its meaning is a mystery.

Probably Raleigh's best-known attempt to form a colony took place in 1585. He sent 108 men to Roanoke Island in what is today the state of North Carolina. The settlers built houses and a fort called Fort Raleigh. Many of the settlers became ill and died. The survivors returned to England in 1586.

In 1587 Raleigh tried to settle Virginia again. He sent a group of 116 colonists, including men, women, and children, to Roanoke Island. On August 18, 1587, the first English child was born in North America.

Her name was Virginia Dare. The governor of Roanoke, John White, went back to England for supplies. He couldn't get back to Roanoke until 1590. By the time he returned to Roanoke, the settlers had vanished. Their cabins were gone, and weeds had sprouted everywhere. To this day, no one knows where the settlers went or what happened to them. Their disappearance remains a mystery.

Raleigh's efforts weren't wasted. Although he was never able to build a permanent settlement in North America, the voyages he organized helped pave the way for others. His crews claimed the eastern portion of North America for England. They also took valuable information about the area's rich soil and pleasant climate back to England. They recommended Chesapeake Bay in present-day Virginia as a good place to settle. In 1607, 104 settlers followed that advice. They created Jamestown, England's first lasting settlement in North America.

By this time Raleigh's life had taken a number of turns—some good, some bad. He helped uncover a plot to assassinate the queen in 1586. She rewarded him with more land in Ireland.

In 1587 the baptism of the first English baby born in Roanoke was cause for celebration.

Raleigh helped gather a fleet of ships to defend his country. In 1588 Spain's king sent 130 ships and 19,000 troops to attack England. With Raleigh leading the way, the English destroyed most of the Spanish Armada, as the Spanish fleet was called. This victory made England the strongest sea power in the world.

Raleigh's crews continued to explore North America. They took interesting new items, such as potatoes, back to England. Raleigh planted potatoes on his estate in Ireland in 1589. No one would eat them at first, but over the years, the potato became the chief food of the Irish.

Sir Walter Raleigh and his son Walter, known as Wat, pose for a portrait in 1603.

Raleigh was most powerful in 1590. Then he made the queen angry. He fell in love and secretly married Elizabeth Throckmorton, one of the queen's companions. Raleigh and Bess, as she was called, had a child in 1592. It was then that the queen discovered the two were married. She was furious because she had not given the couple permission to marry. At the time, the queen had to give her approval for anything that people in her household did. The queen threw Raleigh in prison for almost six months.

Two years later Raleigh came up with a plan to get back some of the money he had spent on his expeditions. He decided to hunt for gold in present-day Guyana (gy•AH•nuh), a country in South America. In 1595 he set sail with four ships and 300 men. He found little gold, but he did take back memories of the beauty of the region and wrote a book about it.

One of the ships that fought off the Spanish Armada was the *Ark Royal*. It had four huge masts and a crew of 270.

The next year found Raleigh and two other commanders attacking the Spanish port of Cadiz with more than 100 ships. The English won that battle, but a cannonball shattered Raleigh's leg. Back in England, he limped into Queen Elizabeth's palace. She rewarded his bravery by making him the captain of her guards again.

While searching for gold in South America, Raleigh burned San Joseph, the capital of Trinidad, a Spanish colony. He also captured the governor, Don Antonio de Berrio, who was finally freed in exchange for a wounded Englishman.

Queen Elizabeth died in 1603. The new king, James I, did not trust Raleigh. He accused Raleigh of plotting against him. Raleigh was sentenced to death, but King James imprisoned him in the Tower of London instead. There he lived for 12 years with Bess, their two sons, and their servants. Raleigh spent the time working on his writing. He wrote a *History of the World*, which was printed in 1614, but it only went up to the second century B.C. He also wrote poetry and a book about his exploration of present-day Guyana. These works earned him a great deal of respect.

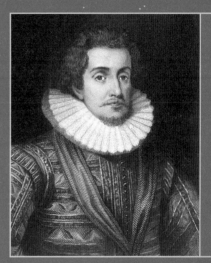

King James I

In 1616 King James released Raleigh from prison. He sent Raleigh back to South America to look for gold. The king gave Raleigh strict orders. He told the explorer not to invade Spanish territory. Raleigh and his crew didn't listen. During an attack on a Spanish settlement, Raleigh's son Wat was killed. Raleigh had to return to England.

When Raleigh reached home, he received terrible news. The king was furious with Raleigh for disobeying his orders, and he sentenced him to death. Raleigh acted bravely to the end. The memory of Raleigh's lifetime of achievement lives on, as does the impact he had on his times.

How to Speak Elizabethan English

American English might sound strange to people who lived during the reign of Elizabeth I. Here are some samples of the way people like Raleigh spoke:

"How art thou?" ("How are you?")

"What wouldst thou have of me?" ("What do you want me to do?")

"I like thy face." ("You're good-looking.")

"I will go with thee." ("I'll go with you.")

"Thou art a rogue." ("You're dishonest but kind of likeable.")

"I am going to the shops." ("I'm going shopping.")